MOTHERLY LOVE

PARIAH

THE FIRST WARNING

To my father, who introduced me to Swedish literature, and to Derek, who bullied me into writing in English.

AUGUST STRINDBERG

MOTHERLY LOVE

PARIAH

THE FIRST WARNING

TRANSLATED BY
EIVOR MARTINUS

AMBER LANE PRESS

All rights whatsoever in these translations are strictly reserved and application for performance etc. should be made before rehearsal to:

Theresa Howard Associates
78 Killyon Road
London SW8 2XT

No performance may be given unless a licence has been obtained.

First published in 1987 by
Amber Lane Press Ltd.
9 Middle Way
Oxford OX2 7LH

Typesetting by Oxford Computer Typesetting
Printed and manufactured in Great Britain by
Cotswold Press Ltd., Oxford

ISBN: 0 906399 79 3

"*Sometimes I have seen actors creating much richer characters out of my plays than I had ever thought possible, and at some dress rehearsals I have had to admit that it may not have been the play I wrote, but it was just as good and in some cases even better.*"

August Strindberg: From *Memos to the Intimate Theatre*

INTRODUCTION

Ever since, as a fourteen-year-old, I was first introduced to Strindberg at the Gothenburg Civic Theatre, where I watched a production of *Master Olof*, completely spellbound, I have been fascinated by this versatile poet, novelist and playwright. It seems to me that Strindberg's greatest misfortune has been to be compared with Ibsen, who was twenty years his senior. As writers these Scandinavian colleagues had very little in common but one play by Ibsen frequently prompted an angry comment in the form of another play or short story by Strindberg. Whereas one could be justified in calling Ibsen's plays naturalistic, Strindberg's plays defy any such generalised description. They span a period of forty years and cover the naturalist, symbolist and expressionist movements. But it is through his naturalist plays that he is best known outside Sweden; unfortunately, these taut marital dramas have reinforced the image of Strindberg as a misogynist. In his later plays, *Ett drömspel* (*A Dreamplay*), *Svarta handsken* (*The Black Glove*) and *Oväder* (variously known as *Squall*, *Stormy Weather* or *Thunder in the Air*), for example, a much gentler, more compassionate Strindberg emerges.

Moderskärlek (*Motherly Love*), *Paria* (*Pariah*) and *Första varningen* (*The First Warning*) were all written around the time Strindberg's first marriage was coming to a dramatic end. He had hit upon the idea of starting a small Scandinavian touring company. "All I need is a table and two chairs and the greatest conflicts that life can offer," he said. "There is one key scene in every good play. That is the one that interests me; why bother with the rest of the rubbish and drag in six or eight more actors?" In the general excitement he and his wife Siri were temporarily reunited and she was appointed *directrice* and *première actrice* of the company. They were due to open with *Miss Julie* in Copenhagen in the spring of 1889 but the play was banned by the censor after the dress rehearsal and they were forced to replace it with another, recently completed play, *Pariah*, which was put on at very short notice. Unlike most of Strindberg's plays, it was well received from the beginning. *Pariah* was the second in a series of nine one-act plays that Strindberg wrote between 1888 and 1892 with his own company in mind. He had to wait until 1907, however, before his Intimate Theatre materialised but by that time he had an impressive collection of chamber plays ready for production.

Pariah is based on a short story written by a friend of Strindberg but there are also echoes of Edgar Allan Poe and Nietzsche in it. Strindberg had just entered into a correspondence in Latin and French with Nietzsche around this time. The main theme in this intense little play is crime and punishment, guilt and redemption.

Motherly Love and *The First Warning* were both written in the spring of 1892, when Siri and Strindberg were finally separated; a drawn-out battle about who should have the custody of the children had ended in Siri's favour. Siri had moved in with a girl-friend after the separation and Strindberg, in a fit of jealousy, suspected them of having a lesbian relationship (something which has subsequently been disproved by the couple's eldest daughter Karin).

The First Warning takes a very light-hearted, almost farcical view of jealousy. In this play Strindberg shows that he is capable of a great deal of self-mockery and irony. "The husband who is in love with his wife is in a terrible predicament", complains the jealous husband. *The First Warning* was scheduled to open at the Royal Dramatic Theatre in Stockholm in 1892 but half-way through the rehearsals the actors boycotted the play because they found it too shocking.

An adaptation of a translation of *The First Warning* from 1914 was produced at a fringe theatre in London under another title a few years ago but apart from that none of these plays had been professionally staged in England before the production at the Gate Theatre in 1985.

Eivor Martinus, 1986

These three short plays by August Strindberg in a new English translation by Eivor Martinus were first presented at the Gate Theatre, Notting Hill, London on 2 September 1985. They were directed by Derek Martinus and David Graham Young with the following cast:

MOTHERLY LOVE

MOTHER (AMÉLIE): .... Valerie Sarruf
DAUGHTER (HÉLÈNE): .... Adrienne Thomas
DRESSER (AUGUSTA): .... Pauline Cadell
LISEN: .... Henrietta Voigts

PARIAH

MR. X: .... Geoffrey Collins
MR. Y: .... George Sweeney

THE FIRST WARNING

HUSBAND (AXEL): .... Geoffrey Collins
WIFE (OLGA): .... Pauline Cadell
ROSA: .... Henrietta Voigts
BARONESS: .... Valerie Sarruf
MAID: .... Adrienne Thomas

Decor: Vanessa Clegg

This original production was supported by the Anglo-Swedish Literary Foundation.

MOTHERLY LOVE

CHARACTERS

MOTHER: aged 42
HÉLÈNE: her daughter, aged 20 (an actress)
LISEN: aged 18
AUGUSTA: a dresser

The action takes place in a rented cottage at a Swedish seaside resort. At the back of the house there is a conservatory, looking out over the archipelago.

SCENE ONE

The MOTHER *and the* DRESSER *are playing cards, smoking cigars and drinking stout. The* DAUGHTER *is sitting by the window at the back.*

MOTHER: Come here, Hélène, we need a third player.

DAUGHTER: I'd rather not play cards on a lovely summer's day like this.

DRESSER: Always trying to please your mother, aren't you?

MOTHER: Don't sit there in the sun getting burnt now.

DAUGHTER: I'm not getting burnt.

MOTHER: Well, there's a draught anyway. [*to the* DRESSER] It's your turn to deal. Here you are.

[*She hands the* DRESSER *the pack of cards.*]

DAUGHTER: I'd love to go swimming with the other girls. Why won't you let me do that?

MOTHER: You are not going anywhere without me.

DAUGHTER: But the girls can swim and you can't.

MOTHER: Who can swim or not swim is beside the point. You know I don't like you going places without me.

DAUGHTER: I should know that by now. You've repeated it for as long as I can remember.

DRESSER: That just shows what a devoted mother you've got. She only wants what is best for her child at all times. That's what it shows.

[MOTHER *shakes the* DRESSER*'s hand.*]

MOTHER: Thank you for those generous words, Augusta. I may not be the best kind of person in every respect, but I don't mind saying that I have been a caring mother, at least.

DAUGHTER: I suppose there is no point in my asking if I can play tennis instead?

DRESSER: You should not talk to your mother like that, Miss Hélène. If you can't even bring yourself to play a game of cards to amuse your poor mother, I think it's downright insulting to ask if you can go out with other people.

DAUGHTER: Yes, yes, yes. I know all that. I know, I know.

MOTHER: Now you're insolent too. Get up and do something useful instead of just whiling away the time over there. You are not a child any more.

DAUGHTER: Why do you treat me like a child then?

MOTHER: Because you behave like a child.

DAUGHTER: You cannot hold that against me. That is the way you want it, isn't it?

MOTHER: You've got a sharp tongue all of a sudden. Is it the company you keep?

DAUGHTER: Yours, you mean?

MOTHER: Are you hiding something from me?

DAUGHTER: No, but it's about time I did.

DRESSER: Shame on you — squabbling with your own mother like that.

MOTHER: What about engaging in some more useful occupation? Come and read your part for me, for instance.

DAUGHTER: The director told me not to do that. He was afraid I might get into bad acting habits.

MOTHER: Is that all the thanks I get for my helpful advice? All my little suggestions and ideas are useless and silly, of course.

DAUGHTER: Why do you insist on helping then? And why should I get the blame for something which is not my idea in the first place?

DRESSER: You keep reminding your mother of her lack of education; it's very mean of you.

DAUGHTER: I don't. But if mother teaches me bad acting

habits I have to object, otherwise my contract would not be renewed and where would we all be then?

MOTHER: Do you have to spell it out that we are living on your earnings? You don't realise how indebted we are to Aunt Augusta. It was she who took us both in when your depraved father abandoned us, it was she who fed us and housed us then and you owe her more than you can ever hope to repay. Do you realise that?

[*The* DAUGHTER *does not answer.*]

Do you? Answer me.

DAUGHTER: I won't answer.

MOTHER: You won't answer?

DRESSER: Calm yourself, Amélie. The neighbours can hear us and you know how they talk. Don't upset yourself.

MOTHER: [*to her* DAUGHTER] Put some clothes on and come out on the promenade with us.

DAUGHTER: I don't feel like going for a walk today.

MOTHER: This is the third day running that you refuse to come for a walk with me. [*ponders*] Is it possible? I want to have a word in private with Aunt Augusta. Will you please leave us for a moment, Hélène?

[*The* DAUGHTER *goes out to the conservatory.*]

SCENE TWO

MOTHER. DRESSER.

MOTHER: Do you think it is possible?

DRESSER: What do you mean?

MOTHER: Do you think she has heard something?

DRESSER: No, she can't have.

MOTHER: Anything is possible. Not that I think that anyone could be so cruel as to tell her to her face . . . but I had a nephew once who was thirty-six before he found out that his father had taken his own life. There must be a reason for Hélène's changed behaviour, that's for sure. I noticed a change eight days ago when we were out walking. It was obvious even then that she was feeling uncomfortable in my company. She wanted to walk where there were no people and when we met someone she looked away. She was nervous and quite impossible to talk to and only wanted to go home all the time. There must be a reason.

DRESSER: Do you mean to say . . . correct me if I am wrong . . . that she is embarrassed in your company? Her own mother?

MOTHER: Yes.

DRESSER: No, you are going too far, Amélie.

MOTHER: And what is worse — she refused to introduce me to some of her friends who came up to us on the steamer.

DRESSER: Do you know what I think? She has met someone in the last week. Let's go down to the post office and find out who the latest arrivals are.

MOTHER: Yes, let's do that. [*calling*] Hélène, will you look after the house for a few minutes while we go down to the post office?

[*The* DAUGHTER *enters.*]

DAUGHTER: Yes, mother.

MOTHER: [*to the* DRESSER] It is just like an old dream coming true.

DRESSER: Yes, one's dreams often come true in the end. I wish it were the beautiful ones, though.

[*They exit, right.*]

SCENE THREE

The DAUGHTER *waves to someone outside.* LISEN
*enters. She is dressed for tennis, in a long white skirt
and with a white hat.*

LISEN: Have they gone yet?

DAUGHTER: Yes, but only for a few minutes.

LISEN: Well, what did your mother say?

DAUGHTER: I never asked her. She is so bad-tempered today.

LISEN: Poor Hélène, so you're not coming with us on our
picnic. I looked forward to it so much. If only you
knew how much I love you.
[*She kisses the* DAUGHTER.]

DAUGHTER: If only you knew how much these last eight days
have meant to me. Being a guest in your home . . .
I have never been with such educated people in
my life before. Can you understand how I felt?
When I grew up there were always strange and
mysterious people coming and going all the time,
constantly quarrelling and whispering and nagging each other — I never heard a kind word,
never received a kiss or a cuddle and my soul was
kept in captivity like a prisoner. Oh . . . I am
talking about my own mother as a jailor. It is a
painful business, painful. You must despise me
now.

LISEN: You can't choose your own parents.

DAUGHTER: No, but the sins of the fathers . . . I know people
say that you can remain blissfully ignorant about
the true nature of your parents until you die, and I
suppose that could be true, because even if
someone told you something terrible about them
you probably would not believe it, would you?

LISEN: Has anyone told you something?

DAUGHTER: Not exactly, but when I was at the baths a few days ago, I overheard a conversation about my mother through a partition. And do you know what they said about her?

LISEN: You should not listen to gossip.

DAUGHTER: They said that she was "a woman of easy virtue". I don't want to believe it, but I have a feeling it is true; everything suddenly seems to fit into place and I am so ashamed, I am so ashamed to go out with her. I imagine that everyone is looking at us, men seem to ogle her; oh, it is dreadful. But is it true? Do you think it is true?

LISEN: People tell so many lies. I don't know.

DAUGHTER: Yes, you do know something, don't you? But you don't want to tell me. I appreciate that, but it doesn't help matters. I am just as unhappy, anyway.

LISEN: My dear Hélène, don't think about it any more. Come and see us today and I'll introduce you to some people I know you will like. My father arrived this morning and he longs to see you. I have told him all about you in my letters and I think cousin Gerhard has, too.

DAUGHTER: You're lucky to have a father. I used to have one when I was very, very young.

LISEN: What happened to him?

DAUGHTER: He deserted us, because he was a bad person, says mother.

LISEN: It is hard to know, of course. But I'll tell you something: if you come to our place today, I'll introduce you to the director of the Grand Theatre. You never know, he could be a very useful person.

DAUGHTER: The director of the Grand Theatre?

LISEN: Yes. And he wants to meet you. Gerhard and I have been talking to him about you. And you know how coincidences sometimes can determine your fate — a personal contact, a word or two at the right time. If you don't come, you'll do yourself a terrible disservice.

DAUGHTER: I would love to come, my dear Lisen, but I cannot accept any invitations which don't include my mother as well.

LISEN: Why? Can you give me one good reason why?

DAUGHTER: I don't know. She taught me to say that when I was a little girl, and I have got used to saying it, I suppose.

LISEN: Did she make you promise anything?

DAUGHTER: She did not need to; she just told me what to say and like a good girl I obeyed.

LISEN: Do you really think it would be wrong to leave her for a few hours on her own?

DAUGHTER: I don't think she would miss me, because when I am at home she is always criticising me, but I would feel bad if I went without her.

LISEN: Do you think she would fit in with our kind of people, though?

DAUGHTER: Goodness, no, that thought never crossed my mind.

LISEN: When you get married one day . . .

DAUGHTER: I am never going to get married.

LISEN: Has your mother taught you to say that too?

DAUGHTER: Probably, yes. She has always warned me of men.

LISEN: As husbands as well?

DAUGHTER: I suppose so.

LISEN: Listen, Hélène, you really need to emancipate yourself.

DAUGHTER: I don't want to be emancipated.

LISEN: I didn't mean it like that, but you need to get out
            of this dependence which you have outgrown and
            which could ruin your whole life from now on.

DAUGHTER: I don't think I can leave her. Ever since I was a
            baby I have been kind of welded to my mother. I
            never dared express any opinions of my own,
            never dared wish for anything she did not approve
            of. I know she is like a great big obstacle in my life
            but I cannot do anything about it.

LISEN: And when your mother gives up the ghost one day
            — what will become of you then?

DAUGHTER: I suppose that is the price I'll have to pay.

LISEN: You have no friends, not a single one. And no one
            can live alone forever. You must have some moral
            support. Have you ever been in love?

DAUGHTER: I don't know. I've never thought about things like
            that, and mother has not allowed me to go out
            with any young men. Do you often think about
            that sort of thing? Love, I mean?

LISEN: Yes, if someone likes me and I like him too.

DAUGHTER: You'll probably marry your cousin Gerhard, won't
            you?

LISEN: I can't, because he is not in love with me.

DAUGHTER: Isn't he?

LISEN: No, he is in love with you.

DAUGHTER: Me?

LISEN: Yes, that is one of the reasons for my visit. He
            wonders if you'll receive him, if he pays you a visit.

DAUGHTER: Here? In this place? No, that is out of the
            question. Besides, do you think I would stand in
            your way? Do you think I would compete with you
            for his favour? Sweet, beautiful Lisen . . .

            [*She takes* LISEN's *hand.*]

What a pretty hand, and what a slender wrist you have. I studied your foot too, you know, when we were last at the baths.

> [*She kneels in front of* LISEN, *who is now seated.*]

Every nail perfect and without blemish; your toes are round and rosy as a child's.

> [*She kisses* LISEN's *foot.*]

You are a true noblewoman, Lisen. I am made of much coarser stuff than you.

LISEN: Stop it! What nonsense you do talk. If only you knew. But . . .

> [*She gets up.*]

DAUGHTER: And you're as good as you're beautiful; at least that is how we always imagine you up there with your fair and gentle features which show no traces of poverty, anxiety or envy.

LISEN: Listen to me, Hélène, anyone who hears you talking like that will think that you are falling in love with me.

DAUGHTER: Maybe I am. People say there is a certain resemblance between us, you know — like between a bluebell in the wild and a cultivated garden hyacinth. I see my better self in you, the person I would like to be, but never can hope to be. When you arrived here on one of the last days of summer, you were so fair and white, like an angel; now it's almost autumn and the day after tomorrow we shall move back to town. And then you and I will probably never meet again. You will never be able to raise me to your level, but I can drag you down to mine. But I don't want to do that. I would like to place you so high, so high and

so far away that I won't notice your flaws. That is
why I must say goodbye to you now, Lisen, my
first and only dear friend.

LISEN: That is enough! Hélène, do you know who I am? I
am your sister.

DAUGHTER: You . . . what do you mean?

LISEN: You and I have the same father.

DAUGHTER: And you're my sister, my little sister. But who is
my father? Oh, it must be the captain, the same as
yours. How silly of me. But he is married, because
. . . is he good to you? He was not very good to my
mother, you know.

LISEN: You don't know that for sure. Aren't you glad
you've got a little sister who is past the crying and
whimpering stage?

DAUGHTER: Of course I am glad. I don't know what to say.
[*They embrace.*]
But I don't dare be really happy because I don't
know what will happen next. What is mother
going to say and what is going to happen when we
meet father?

LISEN: Let me take care of your mother. She must be
back soon. Stay in the background until I call you.
Come and give me a kiss first, darling.
[*They kiss.*]

DAUGHTER: My sister! How strange that word sounds . . . as
strange as the word father. Especially when you
have never uttered them before.

LISEN: Don't let us waste time now but keep to the point.
Do you think your mother will object if we invite
you round to meet your father?

DAUGHTER: Without her? Oh, she hates your — my father so
terribly.

LISEN: But what if she has no reason to hate him? The world is so full of lies and gossip and misunderstandings and errors of judgment, Hélène. My father once told me a story about a friend of his whom he had known during his years as a sea cadet. It all started with an officer who had a gold watch stolen from his cabin and the young cadet was accused of stealing it. God knows why. But as a result his friends kept away from him and that made him very bitter, of course. In the end it was quite impossible to go near him. He picked a fight at the slightest provocation and finally he was discharged from the cadet corps. Two years later the true thief was caught, but by then the damage had already been done. The poor innocent fellow was treated as a suspect for the rest of his life, even though his guilt had been disproved. His bad reputation had been built up brick by brick like a house and when the time came to demolish the false foundation the rest of the building remained hanging in the air, like a castle out of *The Arabian Nights*. That is the way of the world, you see. But sometimes it is even more insane than that. Like when the instrument-maker in Arboga was called an arsonist because his place had been burnt down.

DAUGHTER: Are you trying to tell me that my father is not the person I think he is?

LISEN: That is just what I am trying to say, yes.

DAUGHTER: I have tried to visualise him in my dreams sometimes, but then I have forgotten him again. Is he how I imagine him . . . tall, with a dark beard and large blue sailor's eyes?

LISEN: Yes, something like that.

DAUGHTER: And . . . wait. Now I remember. Look at this watch. There is a little compass attached to the chain — and on that compass there is a spot marked North. Who gave this watch to me?

LISEN: Your father! I was with him when he bought it.

DAUGHTER: Then it must be him I have seen all those times in the theatre, when I have been on the stage. He was always sitting on the left side of the stalls, with his opera glasses. I didn't dare tell mother because she was always so protective towards me. And once he threw some flowers onto the stage, but mother burnt them. Do you think that could have been him too?

LISEN: Yes, that was him all right and you can't imagine how he has followed you around these last couple of years, like the needle in that compass.

DAUGHTER: And you say I can see him, and that he wants to see me too? It's like a fairy-tale.

LISEN: No more fairy-tales now. I can hear your mother coming. If you leave us alone, I'll deal with her.

DAUGHTER: I know something terrible is going to happen. Why can't people be friends and keep peace with one another? I wish it was all over. If only mother would be a little more obliging. I'll pray to God that He might make her good. But I don't expect He can do that, or want to either for that matter.

LISEN: He both can and wants to, if only you'd believe it was possible. Trust in your own happiness and your own ability a little more.

DAUGHTER: Ability? What ability? To be ruthless? No, I can't. And happiness bought at the expense of other people's tears cannot be of lasting value.

LISEN: Will you let me handle this? Why don't you sit down?

DAUGHTER: How can you possibly think that this will end happily?

LISEN: Shhh!

SCENE FOUR

MOTHER *enters*.

LISEN: Dear Mrs . . .

MOTHER: Miss, if you don't mind.

LISEN: Your daughter . . .

MOTHER: Yes, what of it? I have a daughter although I am not married. I am not the only one and I am not ashamed of it either. What do you want?

LISEN: I came here to ask if Miss Hélène could join us for a picnic.

MOTHER: Hasn't she given you her answer yet?

LISEN: Yes, she answered, quite properly, that I should come to you.

MOTHER: That was not an honest answer, Hélène, my child. Do you want to go to a party where your mother is not invited?

DAUGHTER: Yes, with your permission.

MOTHER: With my permission? What influence could I have over a big girl like you? You must tell the young lady yourself what you want to do. But if you prefer to amuse yourself while your poor mother is being disgraced . . . if you want people to ask after your mother and if you want to admit that she wasn't invited because of this or that . . . go on, tell the young lady what you want to do.

LISEN: Please don't let us argue any more. I know exactly what Hélène wants to do and I can also see the way you are trying to persuade her to your way of thinking. If you're really as fond of your daughter as you say you are, then you'd want what is best for her, even if it might be hurtful to you.

MOTHER: Listen, my girl. I know who you are and where you come from even though I have not had the pleasure of being introduced, but don't try and be high and mighty with me, because you have nothing to teach me.

LISEN: I am not so sure of that. Since my mother died six years ago I have been looking after my brothers and sisters and I have noticed that there are a lot of people in the world who never seem to learn anything from experience, however long they live.

MOTHER: What are you trying to say?

LISEN: All I want to say is: this is a great opportunity for your daughter to be introduced in society, maybe have her talents acknowledged, form a relationship perhaps with a young man with good prospects . . .

MOTHER: That sounds excellent but where do I fit in?

LISEN: We are not talking about you. We are talking about your daughter. Can't you spare her one single thought without referring to yourself?

MOTHER: But when I think about myself, you see, I also think about my daughter, because she has learnt to love her mother . . .

LISEN: I don't believe that. She has got so deeply attached to you because you've always kept her away from everyone else, and she had to have some company after all, when you tore her away from her own father.

MOTHER: What did you say?

LISEN: Yes, you robbed her of her own father who refused to marry you because you had been unfaithful to him. Then you avenged yourself on him by preventing him from seeing his daughter. But it was really your fault in the first place.

MOTHER: Hélène, don't believe a word of it! I never thought I'd live to see the day when a complete stranger walks into my room and humiliates me in front of my own daughter.

[*The* DAUGHTER *comes forward.*]

DAUGHTER: Don't speak ill of my mother.

LISEN: I can't help it if I am going to tell the truth about my father. However, I realise that this conversation is not leading anywhere. [*to the* MOTHER] I'd just like to give you a few pieces of advice before I go. Firstly: get rid of that "flesh-broker" who calls herself Aunt Augusta, unless you want to ruin your daughter's reputation entirely. And secondly: I strongly advise you to keep all the receipts for the money my father has given you for Hélène's education, because you'll have to account for every penny of it. And stop following your daughter around in the streets, but above all, leave her alone in the theatre or she is not going to get any more offers of work. But in that case, I suppose you'll just resort to selling her favours in the same unscrupulous way that you have tried to regain your lost reputation at the expense of her future up to now.

[*The* MOTHER *is annihilated.*]

DAUGHTER: [*to* LISEN] Leave us at once. You don't hold anything sacred, do you, not even motherhood.

LISEN: Sacred! You mean as sacred as when the boys cry "pax"?

DAUGHTER: I believe you've come here just to destroy.

LISEN: No, I came here to restore — my father's reputation; my father who was as innocent as that arsonist I told you about who was falsely accused of something he had never done. I also came to obtain redress for you who are the victim of a woman whose only alternative now is to withdraw to some place where she cannot interfere in other people's lives and where she herself can be left alone. That was the purpose of my visit, so now you know. Goodbye!

MOTHER: Don't go yet. Let me say a few words first. You came here — never mind all that high-falutin' stuff — to invite Hélène . . .

LISEN: Yes, we wanted her to meet the director of the Grand Theatre, because he is interested in her acting.

MOTHER: What? The director of the Grand Theatre? Why didn't you tell me that before? Of course you must go, Hélène. Yes, without me.

[*The* DAUGHTER *gestures.*]

LISEN: So you're human after all! Hélène, you may come. Did you hear that?

DAUGHTER: Yes, I heard. But I don't want to go now.

MOTHER: Nonsense.

DAUGHTER: No, I won't feel at ease in that company. And I don't want to be with people who despise my mother.

MOTHER: Rubbish. Are you going to stand in your own light? Come on, go and get dressed at once.

DAUGHTER: No, I cannot. I can't leave you now that I know everything. I shall not be able to enjoy myself for a moment. I shall never believe in anything again . . .

LISEN: [*to the* MOTHER] "As you sow you are like to reap."
And if a young man should come along one day
asking for your daughter's hand in marriage,
you'll be left behind, regretting your foolish
behaviour. Goodbye now.

> [*She walks up to* HÉLÈNE *and kisses her
> forehead.*]

Goodbye, dear sister!

DAUGHTER: Goodbye.

LISEN: Please look me in the eye and show me that you've
still got a ray of hope left.

DAUGHTER: I cannot. I can't bring myself to thank you either
because, however good your intentions were, you
have done me more harm than you can possibly
realise — you came like a snake in the grass when
I was dozing on a sunny hillside.

LISEN: Go back to sleep again then. Next time I shall
come with flowers and music. Goodnight! And
sleep well.

SCENE FIVE

MOTHER. DAUGHTER. *Later on the* DRESSER.

MOTHER: An angel of light, dressed in white? No, a devil,
that's what she is. A real little devil. And what
about you? Silly cow! What a milksop you are!
Too sensitive by half.

DAUGHTER: I can't get over the fact that you have lied to me
about my father all these years.

MOTHER: Ah, it's not worth talking about. The summer is
past, the rain is over and gone . . .

DAUGHTER: And what about Aunt Augusta?

MOTHER: Be quiet. Aunt Augusta is a very good woman and you are greatly indebted to her.

DAUGHTER: But that's not true! It was my father who paid for my education and everything . . .

MOTHER: Yes well . . . but I had to live too, didn't I? Aren't you being a little vindictive now? Surely you can forgive a little fib like that? Here is Augusta. Come, come, let's amuse ourselves as best we can.

SCENE SIX

MOTHER. DAUGHTER. DRESSER.

DRESSER: Oh yes, it was him all right! Not such a bad guess, after all.

MOTHER: Don't let's talk about that bawdy villain any more.

DAUGHTER: Don't call him that, mother. You know it is not true.

DRESSER: What is not true?

DAUGHTER: Never mind, let us have a game of cards. I'm not going to demolish walls that you've spent all these years putting up. What shall we play?

[*She sits down by the card-table and starts to shuffle and deal.*]

MOTHER: There is a sensible girl at last!

THE END

PARIAH

CHARACTERS

MR. X: an archaeologist
MR. Y: a visitor from America } middle-aged men

*The action takes place in a simple room in a country
cottage; the door and the window upstage look out onto
a rural landscape. In the centre there is a large
dining-table with books, writing materials and
archaeological objects on one side of it, and a
microscope, boxes of insects and spirit jars on the other
side. To the left there is a book-shelf. The rest of the
furniture looks as if it could belong to a wealthy farmer.*

MR. Y *enters, in his shirt sleeves, with an insect net and
a vasculum. He walks straight to the book-shelf and
takes out a book, which he starts reading.*

*The church bells ring out the service in the country
church. The landscape and the cottage are sunlit. Now
and again we hear hens cackling outside.*

MR. X *enters in his shirt sleeves.* MR. Y *reacts sharply,
puts the book back on the shelf, upside down, and
pretends to be looking for another book.*

MR. X: What an oppressive day! I am sure we're going to
have thunder.

MR. Y: Do you think so?

MR. X: Yes, there are flies everywhere. And listen to the
hens. Even the church bells sound thirsty, don't
you think? I wanted to go fishing but I couldn't
find any worms. It really gets you down, this
weather. Doesn't it bother you?

MR. Y: Me? I don't know. I suppose I . . .

MR. X: But you always look as if you were expecting a
thunderstorm, don't you?

MR. Y: Do I?

MR. X: But I expect it's because you are off tomorrow. A
bit nervous, perhaps? Ah — the mail. What is the
news?

[*He picks up a letter from the table.*]

I daren't open letters these days. Only debts, debts, debts! Have you ever been in debt?

MR. Y: [*after some deliberation*] No.

MR. X: Well, then you don't understand how it feels to get these final reminders.

[*He reads one of the letters.*]

The rent outstanding, the landlord making a fuss, my wife in despair. And yet here I am, up to my elbows in gold!

[*He opens an iron box on the table. They sit down either side of it.*]

I've got six thousand kronor's worth of gold here. And that only represents a fortnight's dig. I just need to part with this bracelet to get the three hundred and fifty kronor that I need. And if I were to sell all of it I could afford to launch a brilliant career. Obviously, I would have copies made of the various objects and then I'd finish my doctoral thesis and have it published and set off into the world . . . Why don't I do that, do you think?

MR. Y: I suppose you are afraid of being found out.

MR. X: Maybe that is one reason. But don't you think that an intelligent person like me could cover his tracks? I work up there in the hills all alone, so no witnesses — nobody need ever know if I put away some little object in my pocket.

MR. Y: Yes, but you would have to dispose of it. That wouldn't be easy.

MR. X: Ah! Naturally, I would melt it down.

MR. Y: Naturally.

MR. X: Don't you see, if I were to forge some money I wouldn't need to dig first. [*Pause.*] It is strange, though. If someone else were to do what I cannot bring myself to do, I would understand him absolutely and forgive him, but I couldn't forgive myself, you see. I think I would even be capable of making a speech for his defence to prove that this gold is *res nullius* or nobody's property, as it was lying in the ground at a time when there was no such thing as "right of possession" and therefore it cannot belong to anybody, except the person who first happened to find it because when the present owner bought his land the gold was not included in the price.

MR. Y: And I suppose you would be more tolerant if the thief did not steal out of need but out of a collecting mania, for instance, or scientific interest, or because of the personal glory attached to possessing his own discovery. Isn't that so?

MR. X: You mean that I wouldn't forgive him if he stole out of need? No, you're right, because that is the only time when the law shows no mercy. When a man steals because he is destitute it is just considered common theft.

MR. Y: And you would find that unpardonable?

MR. X: How could I condone it if the law does not? And I must admit that it would be difficult for me to accuse someone of theft — if, say, he picked up an object out of archaeological interest, even if this particular object was found on land belonging to someone else.

MR. Y: So you think that vanity and ambition are better excuses than real need?

MR. X: Need is a much better . . . well, the only excuse really. But that's the way things are. I cannot change that any more than I can change my own aversion to any kind of stealing.

MR. Y: So you consider it a great virtue that you are incapable of stealing?

MR. X: I find stealing as loathsome as it is irresistible to others, and consequently not a virtue. I just could not bring myself to do it whereas someone else can't stop himself. You must realise that I too want to own this gold. Then why do I not take it? I'm simply incapable, I lack the necessary qualities needed and a lack of something is not a virtue. That's all there is to it.

[*He closes the lid of the iron box.*]

[*A storm is gathering. The room darkens.*]

There is thunder in the air.

[MR. Y *gets up and closes the doors and windows.*]

Are you afraid of thunder?

MR. Y: It's nothing to joke about.

[*They sit down at the table again.*]

MR. X: You are a bit of an odd one, aren't you? "A Swedish-American who collects flies for a small museum?"

MR. Y: Don't worry yourself about me.

MR. X: You say that every time I get tired of talking about myself and start taking an interest in you instead. Maybe that is why I liked you so much. You let me rattle on about myself as much as I like. You don't have any rough edges to your character, no prickly temper. There is something soft and gentle about you and you show consideration for others, a quality usually only found in the most cultured people. And you never make a noise when you come home late. And you are quiet when you get up in the morning too. You don't make a fuss about trifles either, you back out rather than take part in a conflict — in other words you are the perfect companion. No wonder we became like bosom pals. But you give in too easily, you are too negative, too quiet. When I started to observe you more closely I noticed that you were full of anxiety. You look as if you are made up of two different people. When I sit here in front of the mirror and look at your back, it is as if I were looking at another person.

[MR. Y *turns round and looks in the mirror.*] You can't see your own back. From the front you look like a fearless man who meets his fate with fortitude, but from the back — forgive me — but you look as if you are carrying a great burden or as if you're afraid of being struck a great blow, and when I see your red braces, crossed over your white shirt like that, it reminds me of a trademark on a packing case . . .

[MR. Y *rises.*]

MR. Y: I don't think I can stand it any longer. Whenever is this storm going to break?

MR. X: Don't worry. [*looking at his back*] You know, your neck looks just like another face, but different from your real one. The distance between your ears is really terribly small. I wonder what race you belong to?

[*There is a flash of lightning.*]

I think that struck the policeman's house.

MR. Y: [*worried*] The policeman's house?

MR. X: Yes, it looked like it. That seems to be the end of the storm. As you're leaving tomorrow, let us have a talk. It is strange — even though your face is so familiar to me, I still find it hard to recall it when you are not here. When I think about you in your

absence I am always reminded of another ac-
quaintance of mine who doesn't really look like
you, even though there is a certain resemblance.

MR. Y: Who is he?

MR. X: I can't tell you his name. We dined at the same
place for several years and I used to see this blond
fellow with light blue suffering eyes at the buffet
lunch table. He had this incredible ability to turn
up in the thickest possible crowd without ever
pushing or being pushed. Even though he might
be standing by the door, at some ten feet from the
table, he somehow managed to help himself to a
slice of bread! He always looked happy in
company, and when he saw a friend he used to
laugh out loud with joy and hug him and pat him
as if he hadn't seen another human being for
years. If someone happened to tread on his toes
he just smiled, as if apologising for being in the
way in the first place. I observed him for two
years, amusing myself by trying to guess his
profession and character. But I never asked
anyone about him, because I didn't want to know.
That would have spoilt my fun, you see. This man
was indefinable, like you. Sometimes I used to
think that he might be a trainee teacher, another
time a non-commissioned officer, or a chemist, or
a local government officer or even a secret
policeman. Like you, he seemed to be two people
in one and the two did not match in his case
either. One day I happened to read in the paper
about a forgery in which a well-known civil
servant was involved. Afterwards, I found out that
my mysterious friend was connected with this
person's brother and that his name was Strohman.

I was then informed that the much talked-about Strohman had run his own lending library, but at the time he was working as a crime reporter for a large newspaper. What was the connection between the forgery, the police and my indefinable friend's unusual behaviour? I don't know, but when I asked somebody if Strohman had ever been involved in any crime I didn't get a straight answer.

[*Pause.*]

MR. Y: Well, had he?

MR. X: No. He'd never been convicted of anything anyway!

[*Pause.*]

MR. Y: Is that why he was so attracted to the police, do you think? And also why he was so afraid of upsetting people?

MR. X: Yes.

MR. Y: Did you meet him afterwards?

MR. X: No, I didn't wish to.

[*Pause.*]

MR. Y: Would you have made friends with him if he had been in trouble with the police?

MR. X: I see no reason why not.

[MR. Y *gets up and paces up and down.*]

Sit still! Why can't you sit still?

MR. Y: Where did you get your liberal attitudes from? Are you a Christian?

MR. X: No, can't you tell? A Christian insists on mercy but I insist on punishment to restore the balance or whatever you want to call it. You, who have served your time, should understand that viewpoint.

[MR. Y *becomes motionless, looks at* MR. X,

> *spitefully at first, but then with surprise and admiration.*]

MR. Y: How . . . do . . . you . . . know . . . that?

MR. X: I can tell.

MR. Y: How? How can you tell?

MR. X: I have studied the art of the psyche because undoubtedly it is an art. But let us not talk about that now.

> [*He looks at his watch. He places a piece of paper on the table, dips his pen in the ink and hands it to* MR. Y.]

I must consider my shaky finances. Will you please sign as a witness here? I have to hand this document over to the bank in Malmö tomorrow, when we go there.

MR. Y: I am not going via Malmö.

MR. X: Not going?

MR. Y: No.

MR. X: But surely you can witness my signature anyway?

MR. Y: I never sign anything . . .

MR. X: . . . any more, you mean. This is the fifth time you refuse to sign your name. The first time I asked you it was just a receipt from the post office, but that is when I started to observe you more closely; and now I have noticed that you are horrified at holding a pen in your hand, even. You haven't sent one letter since you arrived — just a postcard, written in pencil. Do you see now how I came to my conclusion? This must be the seventh time that you refuse to come with me to Malmö and you haven't been there once since you arrived, although you've come all the way from America just to see Malmö. And every morning you walk five kilometres to the south, to that windmill on top of the hill, just to catch a glimpse of the rooftops in Malmö. And when you stand there and look out through the latticed window you can see the spires of the castle and the chimneys of the county prison. I'm not trying to prove my superiority, but don't you think you've behaved rather foolishly?

MR. Y: I suppose you despise me now?

MR. X: No.

MR. Y: Yes, you must do.

MR. X: No. Here is my hand.

> [MR. Y *kisses* MR. X's *hand.* MR. X *withdraws his hand.*]

What kind of dog manners is this?

MR. Y: I am sorry, but you're the first person to offer me your hand after finding out . . .

MR. X: And now you suddenly want to show me a mark of respect. It frightens me, that, after having served your sentence you don't feel more self-assured, more equal to me. Do you want to tell me exactly what happened?

MR. Y: [*uneasily*] Yes, but you are not going to believe me. When I tell you the whole story you will understand that I am no ordinary criminal. You will realise that we can make these — what shall I call them — involuntary slips. They happen quite spontaneously and you simply cannot help it. May I open the door a little? I think the storm has passed.

MR. X: By all means.

> [MR. Y *opens the door, then sits down by the table and tells the following story with a great deal of affectation and exaggeration.*]

MR. Y: Well, you see. Once when I was a student at Lund

University I needed a bank loan urgently. I didn't
have any other debts to speak of at the time and
my father was quite well off — not wealthy exactly
but — however, I had sent an I.O.U. to the
second guarantor for him to sign and contrary to
all expectations he sent it back with a letter saying
that he refused to sign it. I was stunned at first. It
was a most unpleasant surprise, most unpleasant.
The document lay there in front of me on the
table with his letter beside it. My eyes wandered
desperately across the fatal lines which had sealed
my fate. Luckily, I could easily find another
guarantor, as many as I liked in fact, but the whole
business was still most unpleasant. As I was sitting
there, my eyes finally fixed on the signature at the
bottom of the letter, a signature which could have
spelt success for me if only it had been in a
different place. It was an unusually calligraphic
signature — you know the sort of decorative
doodling one does sometimes on a piece of
blotting paper. I held the pen in my hand . . .
[*demonstrates*] . . . like this, and somehow it just
began to move by itself. I don't want to suggest
that there was anything mysterious or supernatu-
ral about it — because I don't believe in that kind
of thing. It was a purely mechanical process —
copying this beautiful autograph again and again,
without any sinister intentions, mind you. When
the letter was full of this doodling I had become
quite adept at signing his name. [*throws the pen to
one side*] Then I forgot all about it. The following
night I fell into a deep sleep and when I woke up I
knew that I had been dreaming, but I could not
remember what. Something about a door opening

ever so slightly, and I think I saw the desk with the I.O.U. on it; when I got up I was drawn towards the desk, just as if I had made up my mind in my sleep to sign this name on the ill-fated piece of paper. All thoughts of the consequences, of the risks involved, had vanished. I didn't hesitate for one moment — it was almost as if I were fulfilling a sacred duty — and I signed it. [*leaps up*] What can it mean? Was it just what they call a suggestive impulse? But who was exercising his suggestive powers over me, do you think? There was no one else in the room where I was sleeping. Could it have been that primitive part of me, the Rousseauan savage who turned up with his criminal cravings and his inability to foresee the consequences of anything? What do you think?

MR. X: [*admits reluctantly*] To be honest, your story does not satisfy me entirely. There are gaps in it but maybe that is because you can't remember all the details, and I think I can remember reading somewhere about criminal impulses. But never mind, you've served your sentence now and you've had the courage to mention your transgression. Don't let us talk about it any more.

MR. Y: Yes, yes, yes we shall talk about it. We shall talk until I am quite convinced that I am exonerated.

MR. X: Aren't you convinced about that now, then?

MR. Y: No, I am not.

MR. X: You see, that is what worries me. But we all have skeletons in our cupboards and I am sure we are all guilty of lying and petty thieving as children. Well, there are some people who remain children all their lives and they cannot control their criminal impulses. As soon as an opportunity presents itself, they succumb. But I can't understand why you still have these feelings of guilt. If a child can't be held responsible for his actions, why should the criminal? It is strange . . . I may regret saying this, but . . . well . . . [*Pause.*] I killed a person once — and I have never felt any remorse.

MR. Y: [*extremely interested*] Have you . . . ?

MR. X: Yes, I have. Do you want to shake hands with a murderer?

MR. Y: [*cheerily*] What nonsense!

MR. X: But I was never convicted.

MR. Y: [*sarcastically*] Good for you! How did you get away with it?

MR. X: There were no witnesses; hence no prosecution. I'll tell you what happened; a friend of mine had asked me to join a hunting party outside Uppsala one Christmas. He sent a drunken old coachman to fetch me but the wretched man fell asleep on the box, got stuck in the mud and finally drove off the road. I am not suggesting that my life was endangered in any way but I lost my temper and gave him a blow to sober him up, as I thought, but the upshot was that he never regained consciousness at all, but died on the spot.

MR. Y: [*shrewdly*] Didn't you report it to the police?

MR. X: No, I didn't, for the simple reason that the man had no next of kin or anyone else for that matter who was dependent on him. He had come to the end of his somnolent existence and his job as a coachman could easily be taken over by someone else in greater need of money than he . . . I, on the other hand, had a lot of dependants who could not possibly manage without me. Apart from that, there was also my contribution to the world of science. And because of the unfortunate outcome of this blow I was already cured of my desire to deal any more blows, and I did not wish to ruin my parents' lives, or my own for that matter, just to satisfy some abstract notion of justice.

MR. Y: So that is how you value human life?

MR. X: This particular one, yes.

MR. Y: But what about your feelings of guilt? The balance of justice?

MR. X: I don't have any feelings of guilt because I don't think I've committed any crime. I used to receive and deal many blows as a child but the reason why this particular blow became fatal was that I didn't realise the full impact of such a blow on an elderly person.

MR. Y: But what is the sentence for manslaughter? Isn't it the same as for forgery? Two years' hard labour?

MR. X: Obviously, I've thought about that too. And I've often dreamt that I was locked up in prison. Is it as awful as people say?

MR. Y: Yes, it is awful. First they disfigure you by cutting off your hair so if you did not look like a crook to start with you certainly end up looking like one. When you look at yourself in the mirror you are convinced that you are facing a hard-core criminal.

MR. X: Maybe they are just trying to unmask you that way. Quite clever, really.

MR. Y: It's all right for you to joke about it. They reduce your daily food rations so you're constantly aware of the borderline between life and death. All your vital functions are suppressed, you feel shrivelled up and your soul, which ought to be healed and improved in that place, is starved instead, is pushed back thousands of years. You're only allowed to read books written for savages, you're only told about things which will never come to pass in heaven even. What happens here on earth remains a secret. You are taken out of your environment, moved out of your class and you end up below those who should be below you; you have visions of living in the Bronze Age, you feel as if you're walking around in an animal skin, living in a hovel, drinking out of a trough. Oh!

MR. X: But maybe it's justified. He who behaves like a Bronze Age man should also be dressed like one.

MR. Y: [*angrily*] And that is coming from you who have behaved like a Stone Age man and still manage to live in the Golden Age.

MR. X: [*sharply*] What do you mean by that last remark — Golden Age?

MR. Y: [*cunningly*] Nothing.

MR. X: You're lying, because you're too cowardly to complete the sentence.

MR. Y: You call me a coward, do you? Was I cowardly when I turned up in this place where I have suffered so much? Do you know what I found hardest to swallow? The fact that others weren't in prison as well.

MR. X: Which others?

MR. Y: Those who haven't been punished.

MR. X: Are you alluding to me?

MR. Y: Yes.

MR. X: I have not committed a crime.

MR. Y: Haven't you?

MR. X: An accident is not a crime.

MR. Y: So you call committing a murder an accident?

MR. X: I haven't committed any murder.

MR. Y: Is it not called murder when you kill somebody?

MR. X: No, not always. There is manslaughter, homicide, grievous bodily harm ending in death, and all the subdivisions according to whether it was intentional or unintentional. However, what really frightens me about you is that you belong to that most dangerous category of people who are simply stupid.

MR. Y: You think I am stupid? Shall I prove that you're wrong?

MR. X: Please go ahead.

MR. Y: Perhaps you'll permit me to present a rational and logical analysis of the situation. You've been involved in an accident which could have led to two years' imprisonment. Luckily, you've managed to escape this ignominy. Then you have another man who has acted on an unconscious impulse — and for that he has spent two years doing hard labour. The only way he can restore his reputation to its former glory is through great scientific achievement — but for that he needs money — a lot of money — at once. Don't you think it would be fair if the other person — the one who has escaped punishment altogether — were to pay a reasonable fine? What do you say?

MR. X: [*calmly*] Yes.

MR. Y: So you agree. Hm. [*Pause.*] And what do you consider a reasonable fine?

MR. X: Reasonable? The law stipulates a minimum of fifty kronor for death by misadventure but as the deceased did not have any relations there is no point in pursuing the matter.

MR. Y: You don't want to understand, do you? Let me put it a bit more bluntly then. It is to me you are to pay this fine.

MR. X: I see, that is novel. A murderer pays his fine to a forger. But there is no witness for the prosecution.

MR. Y: Yes, me.

MR. X: Now I begin to understand. How much do you want then?

MR. Y: Six thousand kronor.

MR. X: Too much. Where would I get the money from?

        [MR. Y *points to the box.*]

No, I don't want to steal.

MR. Y: Don't try and tell me that you have never dipped into that box before.

MR. X: [*to himself*] How could I be so totally mistaken? But that is often the way with gentle people. We take a liking to those gentle people and convince ourselves that the liking is mutual; that is why I have always been on my guard against people I like. So you think that I have dipped into that box before, do you?

MR. Y: Most certainly.

MR. X: And you're going to report me to the police if I don't give you six thousand kronor?

MR. Y: Certainly. There is no escape from it now.

MR. X: You think that I want to disgrace my father and my wife and my children and my friends by turning into a common thief? No, I will never do that. I shall go straight to the police and confess everything.

        [MR. Y *gets up quickly and gathers his things.*]

MR. Y: Wait a minute!

MR. X: Why?

MR. Y: [*stammering*] I just had a thought — now that I am
not needed here any more — I don't have to stay,
do I?

MR. X: Yes, you do. Sit down. Let us talk.

    [MR. Y *sits down after putting on a dark
overcoat.*]

MR. Y: What about?

    [MR. X *looks in the mirror behind* MR. Y.]

MR. X: Now I have got it. Oh . . .

MR. Y: [*worried*] What is it? Have you noticed anything
strange?

MR. X: I can tell by looking at you in the mirror that you
are a thief — just a common thief. A minute ago,
when you were sitting there in your white shirt, I
noticed that there was something odd about my
book-shelf but I didn't know what, because I was
listening to you and observing you at the same
time. But since you became more hostile I
observed you more closely, and when you put on
that black coat, which suddenly showed up the red
book-cover, which I hadn't noticed before because of your red braces, then I realised that you
had been reading up on your forgery case in
Bernheim's book on instinctive behaviour and
then put it back on the shelf upside down. So you
stole that story too? On the basis of this evidence I
feel justified in deducing that you must have
committed your crime either because of financial
difficulties or for your own pleasure.

MR. Y: "Financial difficulties"! If only you knew . . .

MR. X: If only *you* knew the privations I have suffered and
still do. But no matter. One thing that is almost
certain is that you have been in prison. But it must
have been an American prison because you were

describing American conditions. Another thing is
almost as certain — you haven't served your
sentence here.

MR. Y: How can you say that?

MR. X: Wait until the police arrive. Then you'll find out.
[MR. Y *rises.*]
You see! The first time I mentioned the word
"police" in connection with the thunderstorm,
you also wanted to run away. And when a person
has been in prison he never wants to climb a hill
every day just to look at the prison or stand behind
a latticed window — in other words, you are both
a convict and not a convict at the same time. And
that is why I didn't know what to make of you.
[*Pause.*]

MR. Y: [*completely deflated*] May I go now?

MR. X: Yes, now you may go.
[MR. Y *gathers his things.*]

MR. Y: Are you angry with me?

MR. X: Yes. Would you prefer me to pity you?

MR. Y: [*sullenly*] Pity? Do you consider yourself a better
person than me?

MR. X: Of course I am better than you. I am wiser than
you and I am more useful to society than you.

MR. Y: You are shrewd all right, but not shrewd enough.
I am in check now but you could be check-mated
in the next move.
[MR. X *stares at* MR. Y.]

MR. X: Do you want another round? What wicked things
do you have in mind now?

MR. Y: That's my secret?

MR. X: Let me have a look at you! You're going to write
anonymous letters to my wife, telling her all about
it, aren't you?

MR. Y: Yes, and you can't prevent it. You don't dare have me arrested so you must let me go. And when I have gone, I can do what I like.

MR. X: You little devil! Now you struck at my Achilles heel. Do you want me to kill you too?

MR. Y: You can't. You're pathetic.

MR. X: We aren't all alike, you know. You feel instinctively that I can't commit your kind of crime. That's why you have the upper hand. But if I were to deal with you in the same way as I dealt with the coachman?

> [MR. X *lifts his hand as if to strike* MR. Y, *who looks him straight in the eye.*]

MR. Y: You can't do that. The man who can't dip into that box even to save himself can't do that either.

MR. X: So you don't think that I have stolen anything from that box?

MR. Y: You're too much of a coward. Just like you're too cowardly to tell your wife that she's married to a murderer.

MR. X: You don't belong to the same species as me. I don't know whether you are stronger or weaker ... more or less of a criminal — that doesn't really matter. But you're obviously more stupid than me because it was stupid to forge that signature rather than beg — like I've had to do — it was stupid to steal out of my book. Do you suppose I never read them? It was also stupid to think that you were cleverer than I and that you could deceive me into becoming a thief. It was stupid to think that two thieves could redress the balance and the most stupid thing of all was your assumption that I had built up my life's whole happiness without securing the corner-stone. Go away now and write your anonymous letters to my wife if you like, and tell her that her husband is a murderer; she has known that ever since we got engaged! Do you surrender now?

MR. Y: May I go?

MR. X: Get out! At once. Your things will be sent on after you. Get out!

THE END

THE FIRST WARNING

CHARACTERS

HUSBAND: 37 years old
WIFE: 36 years old
ROSA: 15 years old
BARONESS: her mother, 47 years old
MAID

The play takes place in Germany in the 1880's.

A dining room: an oblong table in the centre, a large cupboard to the right, tiled corner stove, etc. The door is open at the back and there is a view of distant hills, a church spire, etc. Another door, concealed behind matching wallpaper, to the left. A bag is placed on a chair beside the cupboard.

The WIFE *is writing at the table. There is a bouquet of flowers and a pair of gloves beside her. Her* HUSBAND *enters.*

HUSBAND: Good morning — or should I say good afternoon? How have you slept?

WIFE: Very well, thank you, considering . . .

HUSBAND: Yes, we could have left a little earlier last night.

WIFE: You suggested that quite a few times.

[*The* HUSBAND *touches the flowers lightly.*]

HUSBAND: Fancy you remembering that.

WIFE: I also remember that you disliked my singing . . . please don't spoil my flowers.

HUSBAND: Did they come from the captain?

WIFE: Yes, and they probably came from the nursery-man before they ended up at the florist's where the captain bought them for me. But now they're mine.

[*The* HUSBAND *pushes the bouquet brusquely to one side.*]

HUSBAND: Nice German custom to send flowers to other men's wives.

WIFE: I think you should have left the party a little earlier, dear.

HUSBAND: I'm sure the captain is of the same opinion. But as I had the choice between staying behind and looking ridiculous or leaving the party and making an utter fool of myself, I decided to stay.

WIFE: And make a fool of yourself, anyway.

HUSBAND: Why do you want to be married to a fool? I would never choose a silly woman for my wife.

WIFE: Poor you.

HUSBAND: Yes, I feel rather sorry for myself too. But do you know why I cut such a comical figure?

WIFE: No, do enlighten me. Your answer is bound to be wittier than mine.

HUSBAND: Because . . . I am still in love with my wife . . . even after fifteen years of marriage.

WIFE: Is it really fifteen? Do you keep a record of every move?

[*The* HUSBAND *sits down beside his* WIFE.]

HUSBAND: No, I'm too erratic a player. But you who always treat life like a game would be well advised to count your moves. But I'm already going grey so you see what you've got coming.

WIFE: Is that what you're waiting for?

HUSBAND: That's right. I have often wished you were old and ugly. I used to wish you'd catch chicken-pox and end up scarred and disfigured or that you'd lose all your teeth just so that I could keep you to myself and put a stop to this nagging pain.

WIFE: How sweet of you! And when I finally grow old and ugly you'll feel reassured, at least until something else stirs your blood and makes me superfluous.

HUSBAND: No.

WIFE: Yes. Because it is obvious that your love gets chilled off when you have no reason to be jealous. Don't you remember last summer when we were living on that godforsaken island, with hardly any people on it? You went off fishing and hunting all day, developed a tremendous appetite, grew fat and became so complacent that it was almost hurtful.

HUSBAND: And yet I seem to remember that I was jealous of the herdsman there.

WIFE: Oh my God!

HUSBAND: Yes, I found you conversing with him when you ought to have been giving orders. You asked about his health, his plans, his love life, when you should have sent him off to chop wood. I believe you're blushing.

WIFE: It is because I am ashamed of my husband.

HUSBAND: . . . who . . .

WIFE: . . . feels no shame himself!

HUSBAND: That is as it may be. But can you tell me why you hate me?

WIFE: I have never hated you. I have only despised you. Why? For the same reason that I despise all men as soon as they — what is it called now again — love me. That is it. But why . . . I don't know.

HUSBAND: I have noticed that, so my greatest desire has been to hate you in order that you might love me in return. You see, the husband who is in love with his wife is in a terrible predicament.

WIFE: Poor you! And poor me. What can we do about it?

HUSBAND: Nothing. We have travelled around for seven years now, hoping that circumstances might change, that something might turn up. I have tried to fall in love with other women, but I haven't been successful so far. Meanwhile, I've lost my courage and self-confidence because of your contempt for me. I've run away from you six times already and now I am going to try for the seventh time.

[*He gets up and takes out his bag.*]

WIFE: So you were trying to run away from me every time you set off on one of those journeys on your own?

HUSBAND: Yes, but it was useless. The last time I tried, I ended up in Genoa. I visited the museums, but I didn't see the pictures, only you in every picture. I went to the opera but I didn't hear any singers, only your voice in all its nuances. I popped into a brothel and the only woman I found attractive looked just like you.

WIFE: [*upset*] Have you been to places like that?

HUSBAND: Yes, my love carried me to such extremes . . . and my virtue, which made me too embarrassed to . . .

WIFE: Then it's all over between us.

HUSBAND: Because you're incapable of feeling jealous.

WIFE: I have never suffered from that complaint, that is true, not even in Rosa's presence, although she is madly in love with you.

HUSBAND: How ungrateful of me not to have noticed. However, I have my suspicions about the old baroness, especially as she seems to make frequent trips to that cupboard over there, but as she is our landlady and all the furniture belongs to her I suppose I could be mistaken about her motives. I'll go and get dressed for the journey now and in half an hour I'll be gone. But no leave-taking ceremony, please.

WIFE: You are afraid of saying good-bye properly?

HUSBAND: Especially to you.

[*He exits.*]

[*The* WIFE *is alone for a moment, then* ROSA *enters, carelessly dressed, with her hair loose, a scarf tied round her head and chin, indicating*

> *toothache. There is a long tear on one of her sleeves. She is carrying a large basket of flowers.*]

WIFE: Rosa! Whatever is the matter, my dear?

ROSA: Good morning, Mrs. Brunner. Oh, I have such a terrible toothache. I could die.

WIFE: Poor little thing.

ROSA: And tomorrow I'm supposed to take part in the Corpus Christi procession. And I should arrange these roses today, with Mr. Brunner's help. Oh, my tooth!

WIFE: Let me have a look. Let's see if there is any sign of tooth decay. Open your mouth wide. Oh, look at those teeth! Pure pearls, my dear.

> *[She kisses* ROSA *on the mouth.]*

ROSA: [*annoyed*] You must not kiss me like that, Mrs. Brunner. You must not. I don't want you to.

> *[She climbs up on the table and sits down with her feet on a chair.]*

Actually, I don't know what I want. I did want to go to the party last night, though, but instead I had to stay at home and do my homework. Just like a child. And I had to sit on the same bench as all those awful children. But I don't let the captain put his hand under my chin any more. Because I am not a child. I am not! And if my mother pulls my hair, I don't know what I'll do.

WIFE: My dearest Rosa, what is the matter? What has happened?

ROSA: I don't know, but my head hurts and my teeth and it feels as if I've got a red hot iron on my back . . . and I am fed up with life. I feel like killing myself. I'd like to run away, go round singing at fairs . . . I'd like to be seduced by lecherous men . . .

WIFE: Listen, Rosa! Listen to me!

ROSA: I would like to have a little child — oh, if only it were possible to have a little child without being victimised. Oh, Mrs. Brunner . . . [*notices the bag*] Who is leaving?

WIFE: My . . . husband.

ROSA: So you must have been horrid to him again, Mrs. Brunner. Where is he going? How far is he going? When will he be back?

WIFE: I don't know.

ROSA: I see. And you haven't asked him those questions yourself?

[*She rummages around in his bag.*]

But he must plan to go far, because he has got his passport here. Far away, far away. Oh, Mrs. Brunner, why can't you be good to him? He is so good to you.

[*She throws herself at the* WIFE *and cries.*]

WIFE: My dearest girl. She is crying. Poor girl. Innocent little creature.

ROSA: I am so fond of Mr. Brunner.

WIFE: And you're not ashamed of telling me — his wife — that? And I have to comfort you, my little rival. There, there, have a good cry. It does you good.

[ROSA *disentangles herself.*]

ROSA: No! If I don't want to cry, I won't, you see. And if I choose to pick up that which you throw away then I'll do it. I'm not going to ask anyone's permission before I fall in love. No, I'll fall in love with whoever I like.

WIFE: Well, well, well. But are you so sure that he likes you too, then?

ROSA: [*in the* WIFE*'s arms; crying*] No, I am not.

WIFE: [*consoling her*] Maybe I should plead for you with my husband. Shall I do that?

ROSA: [*crying*] Yes, please. But he must not leave. He simply must not. Be kind to him, Mrs. Brunner. Then he'll stay.

WIFE: How do you want me to behave, you crazy child?

ROSA: I can't tell you. But you must let him kiss you as much as he likes — yes, I saw you both in the garden the other day when he wanted to and you didn't . . . and then I thought . . .

[*The* BARONESS *enters.*]

BARONESS: I'm sorry to disturb you but I must get to my cupboard — with your permission.

[*The* WIFE *gets up.*]

WIFE: Don't worry, my dear baroness.

BARONESS: There you are, Rosa. Are you up and about? I thought you were sick in bed. Go and do your homework at once.

ROSA: It's a public holiday tomorrow. You must know that.

BARONESS: Go upstairs anyway and stop being a nuisance to our guests.

WIFE: Rosa is not a nuisance at all. We're very good friends. We were just going down to the garden to pick some flowers. And after that we were going to try on Rosa's white dress which she hopes to wear tomorrow.

[ROSA *exits through the door at the back. She nods conspiratorially at the* WIFE.]

ROSA: Thank you, Mrs. Brunner.

BARONESS: [*to the* WIFE] You're spoiling my little Rosa.

WIFE: A little kindness can do no harm. Least of all with Rosa, who is a very intelligent and affectionate girl.

[*The* BARONESS *searches for something in the cupboard. The* WIFE *is standing by the door. Her* HUSBAND *is seen entering from the left. They exchange looks and regard the* BARONESS *with a smile. The* HUSBAND *has some parcels with him, which he puts in his bag. The* WIFE *leaves.*]

BARONESS: I'm sorry to disturb you, but it won't take a moment.

HUSBAND: Don't mind me.

[*The* BARONESS *walks towards him.*]

BARONESS: Are you planning another trip, Mr. Brunner?

HUSBAND: Yes.

BARONESS: Will you be gone for long?

HUSBAND: Maybe. Maybe not.

BARONESS: Don't you know?

HUSBAND: I never know anything about my future. I've passed all the decision-making to someone else.

BARONESS: May I be a little inquisitive for a minute, Mr. Brunner?

HUSBAND: It depends. You're on good terms with my wife, aren't you?

BARONESS: As good as can be expected where two women are concerned. But my age . . . my experience of life and temperament . . . [*stops herself*] However, I have noticed that you're unhappy and as I too have suffered from the same complaint I know that it will only improve as you grow older.

HUSBAND: Am I really the afflicted party? Does my "complaint" have to be cured? I consider myself perfectly normal and my suffering consists of watching her abnormal behaviour.

BARONESS: I was married to a man I loved . . . you're smiling. You don't think a woman can love because . . . but

I loved him and he loved me too, but he loved others as well. So I suffered from jealousy to such a degree that I became insufferable. He went to war and enlisted as an officer but he never returned. They said he was killed in action but his body was never recovered and now I imagine that he's alive and well and living with another woman somewhere. Can you imagine, I am still jealous of my dead husband! And at night I dream of him and the other woman. Oh, Mr. Brunner, have you ever been in such agony?

HUSBAND: Indeed I have. But what makes you think that he is still alive?

BARONESS: I have my suspicions because of several coincidences but the years passed without any new information about him. And when you arrived here four months ago, I was struck by a certain resemblance between you and my dear husband. You reminded me of him and once my imagination was roused, so to speak, I grew more and more certain that he must still be alive. I suffer from these pangs of jealousy and that is why I understand you so well, Mr. Brunner.

HUSBAND: [*now becoming more interested*] Your husband resembled me, you say. Please sit down, dear baroness.

[*The* BARONESS *sits down.*]

BARONESS: Yes, he was like you both in appearance and character. If we disregard his weaknesses . . .

HUSBAND: He would be about ten years older than me, I suppose. And he had a scar caused by a needle on his right cheek.

BARONESS: That is right!

HUSBAND: Then I must have met your husband in London once.

BARONESS: Is he alive?

HUSBAND: Wait a minute. I'll soon work it out. Let's see, it must have been five years ago . . . in London, as I said. I had been at a rather sombre party and on my way home I got talking to the first gentleman I happened to bump into. As I make contact easily our conversation carried on for several hours and, after I had told him that I came from the same part of the country as he, he told me his whole life story.

BARONESS: So he is still alive?

HUSBAND: He certainly wasn't killed in the war, anyway. He was captured and then he fell in love with the mayor's daughter, escaped to England where the lady deserted him, so he started gambling, unfortunately. When we finally parted in the small hours I got the impression that he was a ruined man. He made me promise that if, by chance, I were to meet you after a year had passed, and there had not been a notice in the *Allgemeine Zeitung* in the meantime, then I was to regard him as dead. And he asked me to pass on his greeting to you by kissing your hand and to his daughter by kissing her forehead. And he begged your forgiveness.

> [*He kisses the* BARONESS'*s hand.* ROSA *is standing on the porch outside the back door. She looks at them, angrily.*]

BARONESS: [*upset*] So he is dead!

HUSBAND: Yes. And obviously I would have passed on his greetings a long time ago but I forgot his name and the whole incident, in fact.

> [*The* BARONESS *fidgets with her handkerchief. She hesitates.*]

Have I set your mind at rest now?

BARONESS: In a way, yes. But, on the other hand, there is nothing left to hope for.

HUSBAND: No more suffering, you mean . . .

BARONESS: You're right. The only thing of consequence in my life — apart from my daughter — was this . . . isn't it strange that we should miss the pain when it's gone?

HUSBAND: I believe you miss your jealousy more than your poor late husband.

BARONESS: Maybe. My jealousy was my only link with that philanderer. But now I have nothing.

[*She takes his hand.*]

You, who brought me his last greetings, are like a living memory of him and you have suffered just like me!

[*The* HUSBAND, *agitated, gets up and looks at his watch.*]

HUSBAND: Excuse me, I have to catch the next train. I simply must.

BARONESS: That is just what I was going to ask you about. Do you have to leave? Don't you like it here?

[ROSA *leaves, unnoticed by the other two.*]

HUSBAND: I have spent some of my best moments of the last stormy years here under your roof and it is with great regret that I leave you — but I have to —

BARONESS: Because of what happened last night?

HUSBAND: Not only that, but that was the straw that broke the camel's back. If you'll excuse me, I must pack my things now.

[*He arranges his things in his bag.*]

BARONESS: So your departure is inevitable. Will you allow me to help you? As no one else will . . .

HUSBAND: I am most grateful to you, my dear baroness, but I

am practically packed already and I must implore you not to prolong our leave-taking. It is always such a painful business. Your kindness has given me great comfort in my suffering and it is hard to say goodbye. It is almost like saying goodbye to my own mother. I often noticed your kind sympathy when decorum prevented you from intervening and I sometimes wonder whether it is thanks to you that my wife and I managed to maintain such a good relationship after all. My wife would rather listen to you than to someone her own age.

BARONESS: [*with hesitation*] Allow me to say that your wife is not young any more.

HUSBAND: To me she is.

BARONESS: But not to the world.

HUSBAND: So much the better if that is the case. Her flirtatious nature is becoming more and more troublesome. And the less attractive she becomes the more people are likely to laugh behind her back.

BARONESS: They already do.

HUSBAND: Is that true? Poor Olga.

> [*He is quiet for a moment. When a clock strikes one, he pulls himself together.*]

It is one o'clock. I'm leaving in half an hour.

BARONESS: But you can't leave without lunch.

HUSBAND: I'm not hungry and, besides, I suffer from travel sickness; my nerves are rattling like telephone wires in frosty weather.

BARONESS: I'll make you a cup of coffee then. You will accept coffee, won't you? And I'll send the maid to help you with the packing.

HUSBAND: You're so kind, my dear baroness. You almost tempt me into a situation which I may later on regret.

BARONESS: You would not regret . . . listening to me. I only wish you would.

> [*She exits. The* HUSBAND *is alone.* ROSA *enters through the door at the back. The* MAID *follows her.*]

HUSBAND: Good morning, Miss Rosa. What's the matter with you?

ROSA: Why?

HUSBAND: Why? Because you have a bandage round your head.

> [ROSA *pulls off her bandage and puts it in her pocket.*]

ROSA: There is nothing the matter with me. I am perfectly all right. So you're leaving?

HUSBAND: Yes, I am leaving.

> [*The* MAID *enters.*]

ROSA: [*to the* MAID] What do you want?

MAID: The baroness asked me to help you with the packing, sir.

ROSA: That's not necessary. You may leave.

> [*The* MAID *leaves reluctantly.*]

HUSBAND: Are you being rude to me, Miss Rosa?

ROSA: No, I'm not. I want to help you, myself. But you are rude because you didn't keep your promise to help me with the flowers for tomorrow's festival. But I don't mind because I am not going anyway. I don't know where I'll be tomorrow.

HUSBAND: What does that mean?

ROSA: May I help you with something, Axel? Can I brush your hat, perhaps?

> [*She takes his hat and brushes it.*]

HUSBAND: I can't allow you to do that, Miss Rosa.

> [*He wants to take the hat away from her.*]

ROSA: No, leave me alone! Look what you've done! You have torn my dress.

[*She puts her fingers through the hole in the sleeve and tears it even more.*]

HUSBAND: Miss Rosa, you are very strange today and I think you are upsetting your mother with your odd behaviour.

ROSA: What do I care if she gets upset? To tell you the truth it would amuse me. But it might be harmful to you, of course. So what? I don't care more for you than for the cat in the kitchen or the mouse in the cellar and if I were your wife I would despise you and I would go away, so far away that you could never find me again. Naughty! Naughty! Kissing another woman.

HUSBAND: So you saw me kissing your mother's hand. I was just passing on your father's last greeting to her. I happened to meet your father in London once and I have another greeting for you.

[*He walks up to her and is about to kiss her forehead but* ROSA *throws her head back and kisses him on the mouth. The* WIFE *watches from the porch, then leaves.*]

Rosa, my child, I only meant to give you an innocent kiss on the forehead.

ROSA: Innocent, ha! Was that innocent? And you believed mother's fables about father? He died several years ago. But there was a real man! He knew how to love, and he was not afraid of it. He didn't tremble when he was kissed and he didn't wait until he was asked, either. If you don't believe me, come up to the attic and I'll show you his love letters to various women. Come!

[*She opens the door on the left and we glimpse the stairs leading up to the attic.*]

Ha! Are you afraid that I might seduce you? You

look surprised. Are you surprised that I, a girl of
fifteen, already know about love? Did you think
that I believed children were born through the
ear? I can see that you despise me now, but you
must not do that because I am no worse or better
for that matter than any of the others . . . It's just
the way I am.

HUSBAND: Miss Rosa, go and change your dress before your
mother comes back.

ROSA: Do you find my arms so ugly? Or don't you dare
look at them? Now I see why your wife . . . why
you are so jealous of your wife.

HUSBAND: That's enough.

ROSA: You're blushing. Is it because of me or because of
your own feelings? Do you know how many times
I have been in love?

HUSBAND: None.

ROSA: None with a timid sort of man like you, that's true.
Do I shock you again?

HUSBAND: A little, yes. Take care, Miss Rosa. Don't let your
pure heart be sullied by the wolves out there. You
say you're a woman but you are a very young
woman, merely a girl really.

ROSA: And that is why . . . why . . . but I will grow into a
woman one day.

HUSBAND: However, as you are still just a girl, I suggest we
postpone this conversation until such a date. Let's
shake hands on it, Miss Rosa.

ROSA: [crying with anger] Never! Never! You . . .

HUSBAND: Are we going to part as friends? Please. We who
have spent so many pleasant days together during
this long dull winter.

[The WIFE enters with a tray. She is a little
embarrassed and pretends not to notice ROSA.]

WIFE: I thought you might like a cup of coffee before you leave.

> [ROSA *goes to take the tray away from the* WIFE.]

Thank you, dear. I can manage.

> [*The* HUSBAND *looks at his* WIFE *enquiringly.*]

HUSBAND: That was nice of you.

WIFE: [*without looking at him*] I am glad you . . .

ROSA: Maybe I should say goodbye now, Mr. Brunner.

HUSBAND: So you're leaving me, Miss Rosa.

ROSA: I expect so . . . [*hinting at the* WIFE] . . . she must be angry with me.

WIFE: Me? No, my dear, whatever . . .

ROSA: You promised to help me with my dress.

WIFE: Not just now. You can see that I am busy . . . or perhaps you would prefer to keep my husband company while I attend to your dress!

HUSBAND: Olga!

WIFE: Yes, what?

> [ROSA *puts her finger in her mouth, embarrassed and angry.*]

Go and put some suitable clothes on if you intend to come down to the station to see Mr. Brunner off. And take your flowers with you in case you feel like throwing flowers as a parting gesture . . .

HUSBAND: You are cruel, Olga.

> [ROSA *curtseys.*]

ROSA: Goodbye, Mr. Brunner.

> [*The* HUSBAND *takes* ROSA*'s hand.*]

HUSBAND: Farewell, Miss Rosa. Look after yourself and I hope you grow into a big girl soon.

> [ROSA *picks up her flowers.*]

ROSA: Goodbye, Mrs. Brunner.

> [*The* WIFE *doesn't answer.*]

Goodbye.

> [ROSA *runs out. The* WIFE *and* HUSBAND *are both embarrassed. The* WIFE *avoids looking at him.*]

WIFE: Can I do anything for you?

HUSBAND: No, thank you. I am nearly finished.

WIFE: You have so many volunteers.

HUSBAND: Let me have a look at you.

> [*He wants to touch her head but the* WIFE *frees herself.*]

WIFE: Don't!

HUSBAND: What is the matter?

WIFE: I suppose you think I am jealous?

HUSBAND: I believe you are — now that you mention it.

WIFE: Jealous of a school-girl like that! Oh, my God.

HUSBAND: The object of your jealousy is of no importance. I was even jealous of a herdsman, if you remember. So you were watching . . .

WIFE: . . . when you kissed her, yes.

HUSBAND: It was she who kissed me.

WIFE: Shameless hussy! Girls like her are like monkeys.

HUSBAND: Who ape their elders, yes.

WIFE: You seem to enjoy all the attention you are getting, anyway.

HUSBAND: I am not used to such luxuries.

WIFE: Not from young ladies perhaps, but older women don't seem to make you quite so bashful.

HUSBAND: You saw that as well?

WIFE: No, but Rosa told me. You are a real womaniser, aren't you?

HUSBAND: Apparently. A pity I can't profit from it.

WIFE: You're soon free to choose a younger and prettier wife.

HUSBAND: No, I am not.

WIFE: Yes, I am old and ugly now.

HUSBAND: I don't understand. What has happened? Let me have a look at you.

[*The* WIFE *hides her head in his arms.*]

WIFE: No, you must not look at me.

HUSBAND: What on earth is this? You can't seriously be jealous of a young school-girl and an old widow . . .

WIFE: I have broken one of my front teeth! Don't look at me.

HUSBAND: You little baby, you. We cry when we cut our first tooth and we cry when we lose our first tooth, too.

WIFE: And now you'll leave me.

HUSBAND: No I won't. [*closes his bag*] Tomorrow we shall both go to Augsburg to buy you a new gold tooth.

WIFE: And we'll never come back here again.

HUSBAND: Never, unless you want to.

WIFE: Have you got over your pangs now?

HUSBAND: Yes, but things may be different in a week's time.

[*The* BARONESS *enters with a tray.*]

BARONESS: I'm sorry. I thought . . .

HUSBAND: Thank you, but I have already had some coffee. However, as you've been so kind . . . I'll have another cup.

[ROSA *is standing in the doorway.*]

And if you and Miss Rosa want to join us you are most welcome . . . because my wife and I will be leaving by the first train tomorrow morning.

THE END